LIFE, LOVE, AND DEATH

POETRY OF DANIEL DARMODY

DANIEL T. DARMODY

Life, Love, and Death
Copyright © 2023 by Daniel T. Darmody

ISBN: (Paperback)   978-1639455607
           (Hardback)   978-1639455614
           (e-book)   978-1639455621

Writers' Branding Revised Date: 5/19/2023

Writers' Branding
+1 (877) 608-6550
www.writersbranding.com
media@writersbranding.com

Contents

I am Lost Without your Light

This is not an easy poem to write because I lost my wife
She was the recipient of my love and the love of my life
She and I were interconnected, so we knew what the other would say
When she died and left this realm, it was a dark, dark day.
I loved her and she loved me, but it wasn't all a bed of roses
Sometimes we fought about some absurd thing, and we went noses to noses
But we never went to bed mad because we would both say we were contrite
Before we went to sleep and told each other good night
My heart has been an open wound since she left me alone
I would like to say that in all these months I have grown,
But since feel like I am adrift all by myself with no one to save me
I just think of the great life we had together can't you see
No one knew me like Jean and loved me anyway
We had fights but she would find a way to make me stay
We worked hard to understand and love each other
No one is left on whose shoulder I can cry, not even my mother
I wish that writing this poem would be not so hard
But if it wasn't, I could just buy a grieving card
No one else can say what I say
And nothing that simple can make the pain go away
I want to tell her and let her know I won't forget
And our life together I could never regret
I will love you forever, my dear
Sorry if I was such a pain in the rear

WINGS OF A DOVE

HEARTS AND FLOWERS
ARE OBJECTS OF THE HOUR,
BUT VALENTINE'S DAY IS
NOTHING BUT A SYMBOL
OF OUR LOVE.

GIFTS ARE MERE THINGS
LIKE DIAMONDS AND RINGS,
BUT OUR LIFE TOGETHER
IS LIKE A SHOWER OF
GOLD FROM ABOVE.

I CAN'T PUT A VALUE ON
HOW I FEEL.
I JUST KNOW THAT IT
IS REAL.
I LOVE YOU TODAY AND WILL
UNTIL OUR SOULS FLY AWAY ON THE
WINGS OF A DOVE

The Flight of the Surfing Pelicans

The sun was sinking into the west,
the place we've found to be the best,
and we were watching the surfer's troll
for waves and curls to make them roll,
when all at once they flew our way.
The sight was awesome, I must say.
They swooped along in a group of five,
they made us glad to be alive.
They rode the crest like surfers do,
how they careened so effortlessly we haven't a clue.
The surfing pelicans we'll never forget
caught another wave, on that you can bet.
Surf on, feathered five, north by the ocean,
we'll come back to see you when we've got the notion.

Our Boy

Our boy was so loving, he was so much fun,
When I came home, he would come at a run.
His fur was soft and shiny black,
we miss him so much, we want him back.

Our boy was so friendly, our neighbors would say,
"Give him to us if you give him away!"
There are many who say, "He was only a cat!"
But what do they know, he was much more than that.

It's hard to explain how strong was our love,
he was so special, a gift from above.
A heaven for animals? My God has one.
Our boy will be waiting when our time is done.

God will watch over him, he brought us such joy;
How could God not love our little boy?
If God loves the innocent, the meek, and the mild,
there is simply no way God won't love our child.

We miss you so much, Maverick our boy,
It is hard to imagine where we'll find such joy.
Goodbye, Mr. Maverick, come back if you can,
We both love you, our little man.

Prima! Prima! Prima! My Dear!

Prima! Primal Prima! My Dear!
I call your name, but you're not here.
I need to see your cute grey and white face.
Please don't leave me alone in this place.

Is that you on the fence with a dirty pink collar?
Or are you farther away so I must holler?
Prima! Prima! Prima! My Dear!
I call still louder but you're not here.

I miss your belly; I miss your fur like a bunny.
I'm calling really loud and it isn't funny!
Munchkin is looking for you everywhere!
I keep on calling but you're not here.

Prima! Primal! Prima! My Dear!
I call your name, but you're not here.
Are you stalking a rat or a really big mouse?
Quit all the hunting and come in the house!

No more warm cuddles from the sweetest little baby
If I keep on calling, can you hear me maybe?
Prima! Prima! Prima! My Dear!
I call your name but you're not here!

Why did you leave, where did you go?
There is hole in my heart, because I miss you so!
I miss your chortle to tell me you're here.
I miss the pitter patter of you running so clear.

Prima! Prima! Prima! My Dear!
I call your name, but you're not here!
It's not like before because you're gone to stay!
I will miss you so much each and every day!

The Floofest Girl in the World
(In memory of "Isabella")

Oh floofy, floofy, floofy one,
having you with us was so much fun.
From smuggling up to your "acrocat" ways,
your memory will be with us for the rest of our days.

Your golden floofy, floofy fur
made everyone stop and say, "Look at her!"
Your beautiful green eyes that shone with light
will fill our memories in the dark of the night.

When you went flouncing across the floor,
our life would be lighter and our hearts would all soar.
To say that we loved you is just not enough,
not having you with us is what's really tough.

You knew how to climb, you "grappler girl,"
I just can't imagine where we'll find such a pearl.
Oh floofy, floofy, floofy, floof,
we'll miss your sweet face peeking down from the roof.

Your time with us was much too brief,
which is why we're filled with so much grief.
Our lives were blessed the day you came here,
we all will sure miss you, Isabella, my dear

Magnetic Personalities

There are many unexplained,
irresistible forces in the
universe that we view,
One of those forces has
drawn me to you.

I couldn't explain it
If I tried for a year,
But the desire to be
close to you is perfectly
clear.

I think about you more
than I say,
I imagine your image
every day.

I've opened myself up
one more time,
So how about being my
Valentine?

Eleven Forty-Two and I Love You

The times we shared, how much you cared,
are the things that I'll always remember,
the way you laughed, your eyes of blue.
Eleven forty-two and I love you.

Destiny made you the one
that would create me as your son,
and teach me things as good as gold,
the way you laughed, your spirit did too.
Eleven forty-two and I love you.

The woman you picked to be my mother,
I could never wish for any other.
You were wed, she became your wife.
The way you laughed; you laugh anew.
Eleven forty-two and I love you.

Your spirit departed and flew away,
you came again that fateful day
when I was down and feeling blue.
The way you laughed, your eyes I knew.
Eleven forty-two and I love you.

An Angel Has Returned to Heaven

My mother Pearline was one of a kind
Now that she's gone she stays on my mind
I was so blessed that she was my source
Along with my father who is with her of course

The best mother in the world may sound like too much
But if you knew her you wouldn't feel such
Everywhere we went the neighbors would arrive
Because they could sense that with her love they would thrive

Coffee and advice she always would give
And I truly believe she helped them to live
When we left to move to new towns
Their smiles always turn upside down

The best cook in the world my friends would say
"I wish my mother could cook that way"
"You are so lucky to have her with you"
I knew every word they said was so true

Whether kissing my wounds or combing my hair
The love of my mother was always there
She did nothing wrong in my eyes
If anyone said she did I knew they were lies

Last night she returned to the Heaven above
I don't know how I'll live without her love
Now they are the lucky ones for she is there
Along with the angels with whom she can share

My Love Has Gone Away

The day I found her will always be there
She was so tiny with green eyes and red hair
She fit in my hand when I brought her home to live
I never knew I had so much love to give

She brought such love, joy, and life
But now she is gone, and all that's left is strife
The only way through is to put one foot in front of the other
She will always be missed by me and her mother

We will remember the good stuff and throw out the bad
The best day of my life was when I became her dad
She was a part of my soul like no other girl
Without her now, my head is in a whirl

The sun is shining, the birds they sing
It doesn't lighten my soul, so they don't mean a thing
Her love was complete and so was mine
Without her here things cannot be fine

She loved to snuggle and so did I
I still don't understand why she had to die
It's simply not fair that we live longer than they
I have faith in the end it will turn out OK

All my terms of endearment that I created for her
Fill my heart and make my eyes blur
I have other cats that I will always love
But Munchkin my Snugglicious will look down from above

You Complete Us

Life was normal or so we thought.
We plodded through life without thinking a lot
of what we were missing or what we might have had
if we had children and they a Mom and Dad.
Then you came along and shook our world 'round.
When it stopped spinning, we were left with the sound
of the voices of love and the faces to share,
We go around now like we're walking on air.
Now we have you, our family so sweet.
You fill our lives and make us complete.
We love you now, but surely that grows.
how much more we can love you only God knows.
Thank you so much for giving us love.
We love you so much, you're a gift from above.

      Love You,
      Mom and Dad

At Long Last Found
(For Johnny from your Mother)

I looked for you in so many ways.
I looked for you both nights and days.
I looked for you both high and low.
I looked for you, this you should know.

The pain I felt when they took you from me.
The pain I felt was there for all to see.
The pain I felt would not leave me alone.
The pain I felt till I heard your voice on the phone.

I never thought I'd see your face.
I never thought I'd fill the space.
I never thought I'd ever find you.
I never thought the dream would come true.

A miracle occurred the night you found me.
A miracle so clear anyone could see.
A miracle that lives for tomorrow and today.
A miracle of love is what I say.

I will love you now to make up the time.
I will love you now that my life is sublime.
I will love you forever, even after I die.
I will love you forever and tell you no lie.

To Our Grandkids

To our Grandkids we have this to say,
We're going to love you more each and every day.
We look at you and feel tears start,
because we have Grandkids who are beautiful and smart.
May we live to watch you grow and blossom
into wonderful people who we think are awesome.
Your love for us is very special and rare.
When we think of you, life is without care.
For you are our reasons for being so happy.
We'd better stop now before we get sappy!

Love,
Grandpa

Pretty as a Picture
(For Carole Ann)

You're as pretty as a picture
and growing oh so fast.
The more time we have together
the more we want it to last.

Right before our very eyes
you're blooming like a flower.
To brighten even a cloudy day,
you're more lovely by the hour.

With grace and charm to go along
you're quite the shining star.
And as you get more beautiful,
We wish you weren't so far.

To have a granddaughter like you
is very special indeed.
Whenever you want anything,
we hope to fill the need.

Our love for you has just begun.
We haven't really started yet.
But we'll be here when you need us.
On that you can surely bet.

Love, Grandpa

Little Super Man
(For Josh)

With a great sense of humor
and a smile just like the sun.
you're our grandson so special
you're our grandson so fun.

We've known you just briefly,
but we've loved you as long.
When we think about you
we want to write a song.

Getting to know you better
may take a little while,
but we've got nothing better to do
than enjoy your smile.

Your dreams and desires
we'll find out as we go.
But even without all the facts
we know we love you so.

If ever you want to talk to us
you should know that you can,
because we're always here for you
and you're our little super man.

Love, Grandpa

Inky, my Boy

Inky so black that your shadow was lighter
For more than a year you were a fighter
When it was the fateful time for you to go
All I knew was that I would miss you so.

Baset sent you to bring love and joy
Which you did well while you were my boy!
Now that you're gone, I miss your face
I keep seeing your shadow all over the place.

Your presence is felt long after that day
I have been so sad since you went away.
Remembering my sweet, sweet, sugar bear
Sometimes it's hard for me just to breathe air.

Eighteen years with you went by like a week
I'm missing you so much that it's hard for me to speak.
Bast made you for protection, music, and dance
Without you here do we stand a chance?

The love that you gave me still makes me smile
I will join you again after a while.
Time is so cruel when I have to wait
But being with you was always my fate.

May Bast protect you and bring you to God's true light
May God keep you safe until I give up the fight.
May he keep you warm and filled with joy
I want nothing else for my Inky boy.

Magnificent
(For Tuxedo)

Death battered and towed our hearts
Through the wake of a loss so strong.
Nothing could heal our wounds
Until the day that you came along.

I walked by your cage
You stood and reached for me
I knew a sign was given
That our love for you was meant to be.

You came home with her
She picked you up as we agreed
To your surprise, I was there
To fill the love you knew you'd need.

You magnificent cat of black and white
You wonderful friend throughout your stay
You shall be missed and never forgotten
You will be with us again one day.

Tuxedo, Tuxedo our Boy da Boy
To us you were our oldest son
Though feline runs not in our veins
It will not stop our tears to run.

Goodbye, our boy, goodbye
Goodbye today until tomorrow
Come back to us when it is time
When there will be no more sorrow.

Sheba Lady

Sheba Lady, meow, meow, meow, Sheba Lady.
Talkin' about that Sheba Lady
And that lady is mine.

She was always such a sweet, sweet cat
She never would complain
Whether deciding where she sat
Or when she was in pain.

She really liked to get her hair done
Counting on her parents' touch
She lay around in the sun
And nothing bothered her much.

Sheba Lady, meow, meow, meow, Sheba Lady.
Talkin' about that Sheba Lady
And that lady is mine.

We wish we had her when she was small
But that was not our fate
She came to us after her parents' fall
When she was only eight.

We loved her like she started with us
And we gave her such a life
Sheba never caused a fuss
Until she left us in strife.

Sheba Lady, meow, meow, meow, Sheba Lady.
Talkin' about that Sheba lady
And now that lady is gone.

Final Stop
(For Buffy)

She looked up at me with sorrow in her eyes
Almost begging me to pick her up and love her
She was matted and bumpy to my surprise
The bumps began to move in her fur.

She had lost her owners to death's ruthless call
And now fought for her food but rarely won.
Light as a feather weighing almost nothing at all
She melted into me as we stood in the sun.

Without saying a word, she begged me to take her with me
And I knew I could not refuse her forlorn request.
She had had loving owners here by the sea
But her arrival to our home would be her best.

She arrived at our house and wasn't quite sure
If she was safe and finally at home with us,
But when I picked all the vermin from out of her fur
She finally relaxed and started to purr as we made such a fuss.

Soon she was sitting comfortably alone on my lap
A position she often would claim as her own.
I miss her so much I feel like a sap
Thank God that I won't be alone.

Buffy had fur that went with her name
She was blonde like the color of honey.
Her eyes were sea green and too beautiful to tame
I wouldn't have traded her for bundles of money.

A hole is still there in the center of my heart
I feel the pain right now as I write this.
I loved her completely right from the start
Her presence I always will miss.

Love, Laughter, and Lamentation

Primo was big, he wasn't fat,
but he weighed a lot for just a cat.
He loved to be petted, he really liked my lap,
and trouble was brewing, he often took the rap

When he was small (if he ever really was),
he was frightened a lot, loud noise was the cause.
He had such a gentle and loving way,
even his colors were soothing—a nice white and grey.

Raised by my Jeanie he was hardly ever bad,
then I came along and became his dad.
Other men had been near, but none that I could see
did Primo love and trust the way he did me.

When I came along, he was sick and afraid,
I did what was in my power to come to his aid.
I healed him and loved him, he became my friend,
I loved him a lot right up to the end.

Primo made us laugh with his peculiar ways,
we will remember him always through the rest of our days.
Craning his neck to sniff something new,
missing his antics makes us feel blue.

When he let us know through gestures and shaking
that he was sick from the medicine he was taking,
we knew it was time to say goodbye,
for our Primo Dude we lament and cry.

When you get to heaven, which I'm sure is the plan,
look for Maverick, our little man.
He will guide you around and show you the way
so that we'll all be reunited on some glorious day.

So remember our love, our laughter, our lament,
and we'll be together when our day is spent.
We know that you're happy the pain's gone away,
Primo, our Dude, handsome as ever in your white and grey.

You're the Cream in my Coffee
(For Chrissy)

You're the cream in my coffee.
You're the spice in my tea.
You're the granddaughter I always wanted.
There's no one happier than me.

Life is full of surprises,
you're the biggest one of all.
Who would think a big surprise
could ever be so small?

You're my little gymnast,
so pretty and petite.
You're the one who makes me smile,
the one who is so sweet.

With a smile to melt the coldest heart,
you brighten the dreariest day.
I tell you now that I love you.
There is little left to say.

I wish you nothing but the best.
I wish you happiness and money.
But most of all, I wish you to know
that you're my little honey.

Love, Grandpa

Blessed With the Best

Mothers may be many,
but for some there aren't any.
Some are blessed with the best,
others are stuck with the rest.

The woman who became my father's wife
and brought me forth into this life
is the top of the heap.
With her, love is just a small leap.

Whether I was healthy or sick
she's always been with me through thin or thick
I was blessed with a mother whose love
is a gift sent directly from heaven above.

The last thing to say
on my mom's special day
is that I love you, Mother, Dear,
and I hope you'll always be near.

Seeds of Change

We till the soil to prepare for change,
Then plant the seeds and wait for rain.
To get the flowers to grow in a such large range
We work and sweat and sometimes feel pain.

We give of ourselves, then watch and wait.
We begin to feel hope as the sprouts break through.
We pray we did not plant them too late,
Then the flowers bloom in red, white, and blue.

From the Capital, they flow like a river to the sea,
Spreading across America where we have waited so long,
Past the Washington Monument for all who are free
The sounds of joy and tears will fill us with song.

In the dawn's early light, they shine.
We see them and feel the history stir.
America sees it and says this country is mine.
Emotions flow and leave us in a whir.

Change begins with one little seed,
It does not come out overnight,
But the change that has come is just what we need.
May it lead us into freedom's true light.

How Small is GOD?

How small is God
When we split him into pieces
Don't you think it is odd?
On the subject I could write a thesis.

We label and make her fit our needs.
We ask of her to be forgiven.
God takes care of even the ugliest weeds,
Why at our call should she be driven?

We think our God is better than yours;
In a book it was written.
Believing what we're told in tales and lore
And how the apple was bitten.

We cannot see others' points of view
Are just what they were raised to see.
It's time for me to awaken you
To what God wants you to be.

Perhaps you like to be deadly right.
Religion is the drug of the masses.
Instead of towards the light,
Away from God it passes.

To keep you small and hidden in darkness
Is perfect to keep you in line.
I can't believe in all their frankness
That their God is better than mine.

We all are right, we all are wrong,
But we cannot see the forest;
The trees are there in a throng,
God's glory spread out before us.

In every branch and every leaf
God shows us she is here.
She doesn't care whether a president or a thief.
To her both of them are dear.

So put away your seeds of hate
The fruit you reap is rotten.
Learn God's love before it's too late
Remember what's forgotten.

Heroes
(For My Friend Jack)

Heroes don't always wear a cape.
Heroes aren't always at war.
Heroes come in every size and shape.
Heroes might live right next door.

A hero bucks the odds and wins the day.
A hero doesn't think, "What to do?"
A hero doesn't need fine words to say.
A hero could be me or it could be you.

To be a hero, you can't make plans.
To be a hero, you just react.
To be a hero, you make your stands.
To be a hero, it is how you act.

Captain Jack was a hero to me.
He fought the fight as a hero would.
He fought his fight for all to see.
He would still be fighting if he could.

He showed the doctors what heroes can do.
He lasted years beyond the time he had.
He fought like a hero that is true.
His death was quick and not so bad.

His wife and daughter were left to live
With the memory of what heroes can do.
May we always remember what he had to give.
And that we can all be heroes too.

The Best Cat in the World

There are few people or animals whom everyone can love,
But some fit that situation to a tea.
Some creatures are sent to us like a gift from above.
That's how it was for Peanut and me.

She was the sweetest cat on the face of the planet
And if you had met her, you would agree,
There might be some to equal her, I grant it,
But no cat was ever better than she.

I became her "daddy" and loved her much.
She loved everybody and especially me.
Though she was a cat who loved my touch
To me more like a daughter was she.

She was always there when I was sad or blue
She could raise my spirits with her beautiful stare.
With love and affection, she always knew what to do;
She would give me love and always be there.

Beautiful Peanut "butter" with your blueberry eyes,
Who can I turn to now that you are not here?
Who can make me happy when my spirit cries,
"Why isn't my Peanut near?"

Dear Peanut, I love you now and forever and a day
I miss you and wish you didn't have to go.
If there was anything I could have done to have you stay
I would have with great joy, because I love you so.

With Love,
Daniel Darmody
"Peanut's Daddy"

Traces of You
(In Memory of Velvet)

I feel your presence near to me.
I see your bed, your comb, and your hair...
Painful emotions well up for all to see.
I need your touch but you're not there.

The pain is real, it hurts me so.
Why do I put myself through this strife?
It's clear it was time for you to go.
I'll remember you all of my life.

Your shiny black hair and wagging tail
Were there to greet me when I came home at night.
My love for you will never fade or pale
A picture of you remains in my sight.

Is it worth the hurt that I endure
To have had you for so few years?
I wouldn't trade your love so pure
To wipe away the flow of tears.

Black as Velvet you got your name
Your friends they numbered many.
Without you here it's not the same.
For a replacement there isn't any.

No one could ever take your place.
They'd better not even try.
I wish right now I could see your face.
Instead, all I can do is cry.

-For Alan and Courtney Conlon

Tears in His Eyes

Smokey came home with tears in his eyes,
after living beneath a boxcar with maggots and flies.
His fear went away when he saw with great joy
the food was aplenty and he saw his first toy.

Instead of alone, a new family he found,
seven brothers and sisters, the love did abound.
"Tux" was his favorite, the big brother he loved to follow.
Without Smokey here to love, we all feel so hollow.

His cute little face and angelic little meow,
I think back about him, how I'm missing him now.
The cutest grey ball of fur, his butt was so cute,
if he'd been in a cat show, he'd have won all the loot.

I rarely could find him willing to hold
until that last, bad day when his body was cold.
Today the tears that Smokey brought home
were left here with us because he left us alone.

You Birthday, Oh Yea!

Me heard it was you birthday
It time to celebrate and make,
This best darn party and day.
But me already ate the cake!

Me like to give you lots of hugs
And kisses until the party over.
Me tried to bring my good friend Bugs,
But me got mad when he call me Rover.

Me heard you are the sweetest girl.
Me like to see if that is true.
Me would have brought you a little pearl,
But on the way me ate that too!

Me hope you birthday go real good.
Me hope you like me poem.
Me wish I not eat all that wood
Then I could build you home.

Since me can't come so you can kiss my jaw
I sent them other two
Why not kiss you Grandma and Grandpa
While I go eat your shoe!

Luv, Taz
(And Grandpa and Grandma)

Twin Towers

You lit up the New York skyline,
Gleaming at dawn's early light
Your glow shown through the darkness
As day's brightness faded to night.

Your glorious image is falling down.
One morning we awoke to the news so sad.
Your shine put out except in our minds,
By an act so evil, by men so bad.

What we thought would remain
Is now lying in dust and blood.
Our hearts, our minds, and our souls
Can only cope with tears like a flood.

When we think of the lives you held
Our hearts hurt at the pain that was caused.
How could anyone really hate us so much?
Our lives, our loves, and our businesses paused.

Those of us left behind must carry on.
With flags unfurled we remain strong.
We must fight back and stand our ground
And rise against evil in one great throng.

Me and my Honey

There have been many
great loves in time,
Romeo had Juliet
and I have mine.
Ceasar and Cleopatra
Were true loves that faltered
The love of my life
will never be altered.
Where others have fallen
in love with a dream,
None of their love was to last
or so it can seem,
The love that we share
is love that is fate,
We didn't start early
but it is never too late.
The love that we have
is not dependent on moods or our money
our love is unconditional,
Me and my honey.
Today is the beginning
of the rest of our days.

You Complete Us

Life was normal
or so we thought.
We plodded through life
without thinking a lot
of what we were missing
or what we might have had
If we had had children
and they a mom and dad.
Then you came along
and shook our world around.
When it stopped spinning
we were left with the sound
of the voices of love
and the faces to share,
We go around now
like we're walking on air.
Now we have you,
our family so sweet.
You fill our lives
and make us feel complete.
We love you now,
but surely that grows.
how much more we can love you
only God really knows.
Thank you so much for giving us love.
We love you so much,
you're a gift from above.

Love You, Mom and Dad

Stuck Like Glue on You
(For Donald)

Whether riding on your motorbike
or playing in a baseball game;
we will always believe in you
and love you just the same.

I think of how you joked with us
and made us laugh and smile.
It makes us want to be with you
forever and a while.

You can always count on us
to give you lots of love.
When we spend some time with you
we feel blessed by God above.

You came into our lives so fast
it made our heads all spin.
In anything you do in life
we hope you always win.

Just remember when you're in need
we're always here for you.
We send our love with this poem
and hope it sticks like glue.

Love, Grandpa

A Fleeting Glimpse

A fleeting flash of fluffy fur, with glints of red and gold,
a thing of beauty and magnificence, Freddie's story must be told.
He showed up at our door one day, so curious and beautiful.
Our house is a cat haven and feline visitors are always plentiful.

Somehow, he was different though, very clean and sporting a collar.
We found his owners three doors down, just a hop, a skip and a holler.
He came more frequently every day, there was nothing I could say
except "Hi there, Freddie, aren't you pretty, did you come in here to play?"

Just as we seemed to be closer to becoming real good friends,
Freddie was quickly snatched away, and there the story ends.
No more will I see his friendly face; the street has claimed another.
My heart and thoughts go out to Melanie, Freddie's human mother.

Like a thief in the night, he came and went, his coat so soft and furry,
a cat burglar of sorts, a fleeting glimpse, gone in such a flurry.
The souls of our lost little ones will guide him to the light,
and send him back to earth again when the time is right.

Death Won't Leave Me Alone

He hangs over me like a wind-blown curtain
Out of my direct sight but fluttering on the periphery.
He is always there of that I am certain
Like a hen-pecking wife, it's a little bit scary.

I don't see him directly or spot his face,
But I see his actions through the days of my life.
He has taken so many I begin to lose pace
With the losses and emotions that give me such strife.

What does he want with his insatiable appetite?
Is he glutton or connoisseur when he dines on my cats?
I really want to know and I'm not trying to be trite.
Will I know him when I see him in one of my hats?

When he takes away friends and my dad like the trash
Does he have some plan of recycling the lot?
Or does he keep them around like some sort of stash
Waiting for me at the cemetery plot?

I know Death is there just waiting for me around the last bend.
He is patient in his wait and won't leave me alone.
Will I know him at last when my time comes to an end?
Or will he disappear then like a bird that's just flown?

Dear Old Dad

WHEN A MAN LOOKS INSIDE
DEEP, DEEP IN HIS SOUL
AND ASKS WHO HELPED
BE HIS GUIDE
AND DEFINE HIS VERY ROLE
WHEN ONE WONDERS, WHO
AM I?
HOW DID I GET HERE?
WHEN A MAN KNOWS IT'S
OK TO CRY,
OR TO STAND UP FOR WHAT
IS RIGHT AND CHEER!
THERE IS SOMEONE WHO
HAS MOLDED HIM
AND MADE HIM WHAT
HE IS THIS DAY
SOMEONE WHO TAUGHT HIM
TO APPRECIATE A WHIM
OR TO BE FREE AND
GO HIS OWN WAY.
THE ONE RESPONSIBLE FOR
MUCH OF WHERE HE'S BEEN.
THE ONE WHO TAUGHT HIM
TO QUESTION WHAT HE SEES &
WHAT HE READS
THE ONE WHO RAISED
HIM AND TOOK CARE OF
ALL HIS NEEDS.
THERE IS ONLY ONE
WHO FITS THE DESCRIPTION
ABOVE
ONE WHO WHEN I THINK
OF HIM COULD NEVER MAKE
ME SAD.
I WRITE THIS TO HIM

TO EXPRESS MY LOVE
FOR I WOULDN'T BE WHO
I AM IF NOT FOR DEAR OLD DAD.

The End of the Innocents

We see them daily as we pass them by.
We hardly notice them up in the sky.
They are all around us, left and right.
They run in front of our cars in the middle of the night.

We see their faces, but don't look in their eye.
They tell us the truth, because they don't know how to lie.
We do what we can to try and make sense
How they can be filled with such innocence?

With artlessness that we can only strive to obtain
They come into our world and we cause them such pain.
We shoot them, we hurt them, we hit them with cars.
Their deaths most certainly outnumber the stars.

Some feel remorse when they cause them such pain
Some couldn't stop in time because of the rain.
Some offer apologies but others will say,
"If they don't want to get hurt, then get out of the way!"

We see them beat up by their fathers and mothers
If they did it to one, then they'll do it to others.
When did they lose what's wrong and what's right?
How can they sleep in the dark of the night?

They look at us with eyes open so wide.
If only we knew what they're saying inside.
"Please help me. Don't hurt me" is written on their face.
How would you feel if you were in their place?

They don't know what's right or what is wrong.
They don't know how to write words to a song.
They just know that life can be scary sometimes.
They really don't care if all the words rhyme.

To those who would help them with food and with love
Someone is watching what you do from above.
But if you meant to cause them such pain,
It's impossible for you to wash off the stain.

For Humphrey, Floofy, and Maverick, it still makes no sense,
Their deaths were more than loses of the innocents.
The families who loved them will never forget
The way they looked on the day that they met.

Let's care for the babies no matter what breed
Only you really know what it is that they need.
Love, care, warmth, food, and a protective fence
Don't let it be the end of the innocents.

To Patrick McDonell

... RIGHT BEFORE OUR EYES...

Pieces in Time

Across the ages and through the mist of time
When bodies were buried gilded in gold.
Where fables began to be recorded in rhyme
Began a visionary tale that must be told.

Osiris stepped upon the soil by God's own will
And began a journey that searches for an end.
The earth was beautiful, bountiful, and still
Osiris asked his father a companion to send.

God loved him, so fulfilled his request
While Osiris slept God took from his side
A piece that he might mold his best.
Like perfection Isis arrived with the tide.

When Osiris awoke to see such a sight
His soul leapt across space for her to entwine.
Their love was so perfect, so wonderfully right
They couldn't be happier if it had been by design.

God smiled and said, "It is good I will send down another?"
To help them find their mission on earth. It
Set will be a friend for Isis and for Osiris a brother.
Their lives will be filled with love, joy, and mirth.

And it was good for there was such joy,
They could want for nothing for it was all here.
Set loved Isis but Osiris began to annoy,
So Set killed him without shedding a single tear.

Set tore Osiris to pieces and about the earth he did scatter
To hide what he did from God and all others.
Osiris was spread like it didn't really matter.
A cruel fate that should never happen to one's brother.

God saw what Set had done and with anger, he did shout,
"How dare you destroy what I have devised!"
Isis heard the commotion and with a start looked about.
When she saw not her Osiris she was surprised.

"Lord God, where has my love gone for, I feel not whole,"
Isis cried and searched all the earth.
"I see him not anywhere the half of my soul!"
"Without him here my love, joy, and peace are a dearth."

"Fear not brave and beautiful Isis for you will one day be complete."
God said to her gently. "When the circle is joined again."
"On that day, so far away, you will sit at my feet"
"When you reawaken and the pieces you mend."

"To Set and all others the memory is erased."
"You will forget who you are and where you came from."
"Through history, you will struggle and be chased."
"Come back to me not until you hear the sound of my drum."

So Set and Isis were sent back to earth with this story
To be told until all have found their connection to source.
When God is in them and they channel him for his glory
The parts will be united but it won't take any force.

The male and the female reunited again the way it should be.
The Yin and the Yang a full circle they've come
To join with God and live in eternity.
Pure light and love we will have become.

My Love Lies Over the Ocean,
My Love Lies Over the Sea

Time moves too darn slow
When you are waiting for love to grow
In time our lives will be filled with love
With the help of God up above.

When I look at the photos of you at night
It is as if you are here with me to make life right
I cannot wait for your lips to kiss me
So, our love will be for all to see.

When I stare into your eyes
Know I will never tell you lies.
You inspire me more than just emails can
To be a much, much better man.

Those who said it wouldn't work
Will feel like such a jerk
We will prove them wrong
I will write you this song

I commit to you my sweetheart
I send you my love and desire for love to start
To spend the rest of the days of my life with you
Please tell me you are committed too

My love, My Life, My Heroine

When I think about the woman I love
Somebody who fits me like a glove,
I think of someone who knows me.
But she is far, far across the sea.

Distance cannot diminish my feeling for her,
If I was a cat she would know because I would purr!
I pray for her safe travels when the time is right,
I pray for her safety every single night.

It is Valentine's day and I hope for her to understand
That she is my woman, and I am her man
Distance does not deter us for we are in love
We were drawn together by God above.

When she is finally with me here in the States
We will put away our struggles and hates
And live the rest of our lives together in married bliss,
That will remind us of the power of our first kiss.

My love is in a country torn by war every day
No power, cold days, and no children at play.
She has shown me true bravery when faced with danger,
Moving to Pacifica, California will not change her.

Irina, my love, my heroine, my wife to be,
What I want for you is to be here with me.
I will do whatever it takes to get you here.
Valentine's or not I am yours my dear.

CPSIA information can be obtained
at www.ICGtesting.com
Printed in the USA
BVHW030408220623
666151BV00002B/673

9 781639 455607